101 Reasons Why You Might Have a Low IQ

Mike Stone

Published by Black Line Press

Copyright © 2024 by Mike Stone. All Rights Reserved.

No part of this book may be used or reproduced in any manner, whatsoever, without written permission from the author. The exception being in cases of brief quotations embodied in critical articles or reviews. This book is intended for entertainment purposes only. It contains parody, humor, and satire. The author and publisher bear no responsibility or liability whatsoever to any person or entity with respect to any loss, damage, or injury caused or alleged to be caused directly or indirectly by the information contained in this book.

Author contact: mikestone114@yahoo.com

If you think Sleepy Joe, who couldn't draw more than twenty people to a rally, received more votes than any presidential candidate in history . . . You might have a low IQ.

If you thought "safe and effective" actually meant safe and effective . . . You might have a low IQ.

If you have a television in your home and you allow your children to watch it . . . You might have a low IQ.

If your idea of a day out with the family means taking your kids to Drag Queen Story Hour . . . You might have a low IQ.

If you think 23 Baltimore schools not having a single student proficient in math is Trump's fault . . . You might have a low IQ.

If you listen to "conservative" talk radio and actually believe a word you are hearing . . . You might have a low IQ.

If you hate the way professional sports leagues have become woke and anti-American, yet you continue to watch the games . . . You might have a low IQ.

If you spent four years attacking Donald Trump and his supporters, but were first in line to take the fake vaccine when it came out . . . You might have a low IQ.

If you think Chinese weather balloons are the biggest problem facing the country right now . . . You might have a low IQ.

If you think two planes actually knocked down three World Trade Center Tower buildings on 9/11 . . . You might have a low IQ.

If you're unaware that three World Trade Center Towers came down on 9/11 . . . You might have a low IQ.

If you've never heard of or researched the "dancing Israelis" on 9/11 . . . You might have a low IQ.

If your family doctor spent three years pushing you to take the fake vaccine, and you still visit him for your yearly checkup . . . You might have a low IQ.

If you think the water coming out of your tap is safe to drink, because the government says so . . . You might have a low IQ.

If you think white people are to blame for your failure in life . . . You might have a low IQ.

If you think the government has the solution (to anything) . . . You might have a low IQ.

If you think Europe would be a safe and fun place to go on vacation . . . You might have a low IQ.

If you've ever referred to World War II as the "Good War" or to the people who fought in World War II as the "Greatest Generation" . . . You might have a low IQ.

If you're a single woman and you think men are the problem . . . You might have a low IQ.

If the first thing you do after getting paid on Friday is log on to a porn site . . . You might have a low IQ.

If you think the world is secretly run by aliens, the Jesuits, fascist Nazis, or anyone else other than who really runs it . . . You might have a low IQ.

If you've ever said, "Thank you for your service," to someone serving in the military . . . You might have a low IQ.

If you think the purpose of the media is to inform the public . . . You might have a low IQ.

If you think the mainstream media tells the truth about anything . . . You might have a low IQ.

If you know that the mainstream media lies about everything, but you think this one time they're telling you the truth . . . You might have a low IQ.

If you believe the history you were taught in grade school, high school and college . . . You might have a low IQ.

If you've ever said, "America is the greatest country on earth" . . . You might have a low IQ.

If you think race is a social construct and all people are alike . . . You might have a low IQ.

If you feel guilty over something your ancestors did before you were born . . . You might have a low IQ.

If you take your family on trips to Las Vegas or Disneyland . . . You might have a low IQ.

If you think an "informed opinion" means watching "The View" . . . You might have a low IQ.

If you think the rainstorm that ruined your car wash was Trump's fault . . . You might have a low IQ.

If your most prized possession is your EBT card . . . You might have a low IQ.

If you hate Christians with a passion, but can't get enough of anti-pope Francis . . . You might have a low IQ.

If you go ga-ga over Hollywood celebrities, but you've never read the Constitution . . . You might have a low IQ.

If the three most commonly heard words at your family get-togethers are "It's Trump's fault" . . . You might have a low IQ.

If you're an A-list movie star who takes time off from promoting your newest action flick to speak out for gun control . . . You might have a low IQ.

If you use your parents' credit card to buy designer jeans, video games, and Che Guevara posters . . . You might have a low IQ.

If you're a white-skinned, blue-eyed politician who claims to be Native American . . . You might have a low IQ.

If you think the Second Amendment was written for hunters . . . You might have a low IQ.

If your idea of a positive role model for your daughter is Kim Kardashian . . . You might have a low IQ.

If you buy gossip magazines at the checkout counter (with your EBT card) and wish you were Kim Kardashian . . . You might have a low IQ.

If you think we actually went to the moon in that aluminum foil bucket . . . You might have a low IQ.

If you're a guy who needs Viagra to get it up and you think it's Trump's fault . . . You might have a low IQ.

If you're a gal who thinks every guy who approaches you is a creep and every guy who doesn't approach you is gay . . . You might have a low IQ.

If you call yourself a "conservative" and believe that Israel is our greatest ally . . . You might have a low IQ. A *very* low IQ.

If you think anyone who disagrees with you is a racist . . . You might have a low IQ.

If you claim you're not a racist, but you support diversity in the workplace, affirmative action, and hiring quotas based on skin color . . . You might have a low IQ.

If you think "government intervention" means free rent, free food, and a free cell phone . . . You might have a low IQ.

If you think open dialogue means you talk and others listen . . . You might have a low IQ.

If you think it's normal for parents to laugh and yuk-it-up on television the day after their five-year-old daughter was allegedly killed in a school shooting . . . You might have a low IQ.

If you think crime is caused by global warming . . . You might have a low IQ.

If you think global warming is real . . . You might have a low IQ.

If you live in Chicago and are well known at every voting precinct in the city . . . You might have a low IQ.

If you've been dead for twenty years, but voted for Biden forty-seven times . . . You might have a low IQ.

If you think America is the land of the free and the home of the brave . . . You might have a low IQ.

If you think border walls are racist, while living in a gated community . . . You might have a low IQ.

If you're a teacher who hates kids . . . You might have a low IQ.

If you hate kids, period . . . You might have a low IQ.

If you're a teacher who wants to turn kids into trannies . . . You might have a low IQ. You also belong in jail.

If you're mad right now . . . You might have a low IQ.

If you think "fact checkers" are anything other than complete retards . . . You might have a low IQ.

If you visit doctors or hospitals for any reason other than a broken bone or gunshot wound . . . You might have a low IQ.

If you went to see the Barbie movie dressed like Ken . . . You might have a low IQ. You might also be gay.

If you went to see the Barbie movie, period . . . You might have a low IQ.

If you think colleges and universities are anything other than leftist indoctrination centers . . . You might have a low IQ. (Note to young readers: Never, under any circumstances, take out a student loan. And think carefully about attending college at all.)

If every time Trump is arrested, indicted, or served with a lawsuit, you say, "We got him this time" . . . You might have a low IQ.

If you've ever lent money to anyone for any reason and expected to get it back . . . You might have a low IQ.

If you trust anything you see, read, or hear coming from the mainstream media . . . You might have a low IQ.

If you watch movies or television shows made by people that think you're stupid and spit in your face . . . You might have a low IQ.

If you believe that humans descended from monkeys and apes . . . You might have a low IQ.

If you bring your children with you to watch men wearing dresses parade down the street . . . You might have a low IQ.

If you won't touch a bagel that isn't gluten-free, but you let a complete stranger inject you with a concoction of harmful chemicals . . . You might have a low IQ.

If you believe that Jesus and the Apostles were Jews . . . You might have a low IQ.

If you believe that Adam, Noah, Abraham, Moses and Jacob were Jews . . . You might have a low IQ.

If you're not boycotting all of corporate America for their crimes in promoting the stolen election and the fake vaccine . . . You might have a low IQ.

If you let your children read Harry Potter books . . . You might have a low IQ.

If you're a parent who isn't homeschooling your children . . . I won't say you have a low IQ, but you really need to pull them out of school.

If you're eating junk food, fast food, or processed food—food literally laced with chemicals . . . You might have a low IQ.

If you're one of the few people who actually voted for Sleepy Joe . . . You might have a low IQ.

If you're not spending time in prayer every day, and not actively seeking God . . . You might have a low IQ.

If your husband wears a dress and you think he's hot . . . You might have a low IQ.

If your son wears a dress and you think he's hot . . . You might have a low IQ.

If you don't wear a dress because you're a feminist (and therefore not hot) . . . You might have a low IQ.

If you believe the reason you're a feminist is Trump's fault, you have an even lower IQ.

If you think the way to get a date, a girlfriend, or a wife is by acting "alpha" . . . You might have a low IQ.

If you're a girl reading romance novels or a guy looking at pornography . . . You might have a low IQ.

If you think finding your "soul mate" and falling in love is going to magically transform your life and make everything wonderful . . . You might have a low IQ.

If you think Satan and hell aren't real . . . You might have a low IQ.

If you think Barry Soetoro aka Barack Obama was born in Hawaii . . . You might have a low IQ.

If you think Michael Robinson aka Michelle Obama is a woman . . . You might have a low IQ.

If you think we actually have fair elections in this country . . . You might have a low IQ.

If you believe anything you were taught in school, outside of math, music, English and reading . . . You might have a low IQ.

If you reject the Bible under the belief that it's nothing more than a collection of fairy tales, while avidly watching Marvel super hero movies . . . You might have a low IQ.

If you use words like "tolerance," "racism," "equality," "patriarchy," or "diversity" in your everyday speech, or worse, in a classroom . . . You might have a low IQ.

If you support trannyism and the sexual mutilation of children in any shape, way or form . . . You might have a low IQ.

If you believe you're going to Heaven when you die, because you're nice, or because you're one of God's "chosen people" . . . You might have a low IQ.

If you're living in your parents' basement and you believe it's Trump's fault . . . You might have a low IQ.

If you have pictures of Che Guevara hanging in your parents' basement . . . You might have a low IQ.

If you watch four hours a day of television and believe everyone else is misinformed . . . You might have a low IQ.

If you're not spending time alone, practicing the art of solitude . . . You might have a low IQ.

If you think everything you've read in this book is Trump's fault . . . You might have a low IQ.

The lowest IQ of all.

Thank you!

Thank you very much for buying this book!

If you enjoyed it, please leave a review because people do read them. Even a short, one-sentence review will help.

If you did not enjoy it, please email me with suggestions on how to improve the text:

Mikestone114@yahoo.com

Mike Stone is the author of *Based*, a young adult novel about race, dating and growing up in America, and *A New America*, a dark comedy set on Election Day 2016. He has also written the books:

Teen Boys Success Book
Reversing the Side Effects of the COVID-19 Vaccine
COVID-19 and the Mark of the Beast
Covid 19 and Kids.

A New America

On the most divisive day of the year, in the most racially-charged city in America, recently red-pilled movie producer John Duke is about to learn what political correctness really means: marching with the herd or losing everything, including his family.

5 Stars! "A well-written book of an America gone mad."

5 Stars! "More!! Great read!"

5 Stars! "An exciting well-written novel. The author uses no clichés, his descriptions are original, and as a whole the writing is very creative."

5 Stars! "A fast-paced exciting novel."

5 Stars! "Read it all in one sitting. Had to remind myself it's supposed to be fiction."

5 Stars! "I hope this book is read far and wide, because it is the truth."

5 Stars! "You would never see a book written like this in a mainstream publication."

Based

"Ryan Turner was standing alone on the subway platform when he saw the punch coming." So begins another day of high school in Southern California where teachers attempt suicide, race riots erupt in the cafeteria, and everyone strives to avoid the ultimate in humiliation: diversity training.

A young adult novel about race, dating and growing up in America.

5 Stars! "Simply off the charts!"

5 Stars! "Couldn't put it down!"

5 Stars! "Sharp and funny take on the upside down world we live in today."

www.ingramcontent.com/pod-product-compliance
Lightning Source LLC
Chambersburg PA
CBHW032108040426
42449CB00007B/1217